"REVENGE OF THE ORGASM"

(*AN EROTIC AUTOBIOGRAPHY*)

by

G.P.A. THE POETIC UNSUB

REVIEWS

"Forgive my crass interaction..." <u>The Greatest Poet Alive</u> (GPA) writes in the poem, *Stranger*, from his book , <u>The Confessional Heart Of A Man</u>. However, he makes no apologies for his frank and at times explicitly detailed collection of poetry. Not for the faint of heart, this book is one filled with passion and emotion bound to take the reader on a unique journey. Love and heartbreak, of course. But one will find that this book of poetry sets its own rules and stretches far beyond the typical topics.
From Nola Divine

"The Confessional Heart of a Man" was like reading a life story told in different stages in poetic verse - from a man's point of view. From social issues, politics, love, relationships, marriage, and more. I was glad the author touched on so many topics. He was in sync with his mind, and from a man, I appreciated that, and had to at the very least respect it. Sometimes I felt anger through the author's voice. While other times, I sensed an urge for understanding and expression.

I may be wrong; however, I sensed the chronological order of the poetic nature of each page. There were various poems with different themes, some very romantic, while others just told the truth, bold and aggressive. Yet other poetry pieces were controversial and up for debate. You could very well feel the different emotions while reading - whether those emotions were your own or derived from the author's voice and style.

I enjoyed the rhythmic tone and voices I heard throughout the pieces. It's hard to know what is going through a man's head, and by reading "The Confessional Heart of a Man" it was both interesting and surprising. While reading this book, it became evident that men feel deeply as do women, however expressed and suppressed very differently.

I would definitely recommend "The Confessional Heart of a Man" to anyone who likes poetry and to anyone who'd like to read a thought provoking book in poetry style. I'd also recommend this book to any women, especially a Black woman who wants to get in the head of a Black man and understand what's going on inside both his mind and heart.

Tinisha Nicole Johnson
Author/Writer/Poet
www.TinishaNicoleJohnson.com

Author Marc Livingston (a/k/a the Greatest Poet Alive "GPA") delivers in his debut work of poetic masterpieces - "The Confessional Heart of a Man". This is raw, uncut and sincere delivery of some of the best pieces of poetry I have ever read! The reader will be captivated by GPA's journey through life experiences; he has something to share with everyone. It will take a special reader to truly "get it" - to remove all biases, judgment and misconceptions in order to enjoy the lyrically and poetic gift from the poet.

Buckle up tight and get ready for the ride of a lifetime. GPA takes us on a humble and exhilarating journey where he opens his heart and mind to all who are willing to listen without judgment. GPA has an intimate moment with everything life has to offer from marriage, infidelity, racism, family issues, forbidden and complicated desires, hurtful experiences, grief, love and hate to the 10th power, jail life, life's major decisions, AIDS, parental guidance and love, and a host of other metaphorically gifted poems - through the eyes of an extraordinary man.

It is important to point out that GPA also delivers a wonderful interpretation of a female state of mind - something that is clearly not easy to accomplish.

I was so impressed with GPA and each poem and decided to read many of his poems to my husband in a quiet atmosphere - an intimate moment shared between us. We discussed each piece of poetry and continued on our journey with the author. GPA will surprise the reader and take them in a direction they will not see coming. In many of his poems, the endings are quite shocking, yet thought-provoking and entertaining.

Dictionary.com describes the word "masterpiece" as, "anything done with masterly skill", or "a person's greatest piece of work, as in an art." Was this a masterpiece? A resounding - YES. Will I remember this brilliant piece of work in the future? Yes and so will you once you take this journey with the author! With confidence, I highly recommend his book, and I anxiously await the next masterpiece from this gifted poet and author.

Review: 5 out of 5 Beignets
Reviewed by: Sonya
Books and Beignets (BAB) Book Club

Trina Thomas on Sep. 07, 2012 : ★ ★ ★ ★ ★
This book of poetry was everything I'd hoped it to be. Sexy and erotic in a subtle way. I recommend this book of poetry if you enjoy romance. Review for The Book of 24 Orgasms

Joey Pinkney's review
Nov 20, 11

Read from November 15 to 20, 2011

The Book of 24 Orgasms is GPA's (Greatest Poet Alive) second poetry collection. Instead of the "wham, bam, thank you ma'am" type of lewdness people have come to expect in erotic poetry, GPA is not in your face - he's in your mind. This book gives you a thinking man's sensual path to the same end - the orgasm.

Indulging in indescribable indiscretions is not an easy task when classiness is a forethought. GPA's poems are neither vulgar nor vague. They are intense but not nasty. They are indeed graphic yet not pornographic. As a wordsmith, he forces you to be an active reader because each word is used with phonetic and conceptual precision.

I know it is a part of GPA's poetic style, but certain phrases came across as being redundant. Things like "aggression aggressive", "your accentuations accentuate" and "banal banalities" left me feeling confused, looking for a deeper angle. Many times, there were none to be found. I was also thrown off by what I thought were missing words in some of the sentences. I'm sure that this is part of his poetic voice, and it took me a little getting used to.

All in all, The Book of 24 Orgasms is worthy of a read and re-reads. GPA has created an amazing maze of love, lust, desire, fire and sheer coolness. If you like poetry and love the erotic selections, this book aims to please with pleasurable foreplay.

Darryl's Review: The Greatest Poet Alive has done it again. His style of poetry has twists and turns that keeps every poem fresh with various flavors. I enjoyed The Book of 24 Orgasms. GPA's articulation of words describing suggestive and seductive scenes in each poem is truly clever. Eroticism takes on a whole new twist in a stylish way that only GPA can solicit. If you're looking for a meaty book to take up a few days of reading time, keep looking. What the book lacks in quantity, it makes up in substance and quality by the bestselling poet. I found each poem to be an arousing experience. Each Poem is its own unique electrifying story with 24 enticing titles that can't help but draw your attention.

5.0 out of 5 stars **Aphrodisiac Not Needed**, December 30, 2011
By
OOSA Online Book Club "O.O.S.A. Gets It Read!" (World Wide Web, USA) - See all my reviews
This review is from: **The Book of 24 Orgasms (The Lust Series, Volume 1) (Paperback)**

Put away the oysters and green M&Ms. They are no longer needed. Just pick up "The Book of 24 Orgasms." These 24 mind-blowing poems are bound to get you and your lover in the mood. Cozy up together and read them aloud to each other to set the mood. I enjoyed this book. Some of my favorites include number 13 `My Tee Shirt (On You),' number 15 `A Simpler Rhyme' and number 18 `The Orgasm,' just to name a few. I would love to hear these recited live. I give "The Book of 24 Orgasms" a 5.

Dominique rated it ★★★★★

What an outstanding job GPA has done this time around. He is named one of the best poetry authors for a reason. The Mind of a Poetic Unsub is a hardcore straight to the point poetry book that everyone can relate to. That gives you a glimpse of who GPA is, what he's done, where he's been and where he's going. Not only do we get more into GPA but we meet Marc, the name and face that has created GPA. If you have not picked up a book by GPA you must. Anyone who is not a fan of poetry will be after this book. The level of intensity and realness GPA gives is unbelievable.

African Americans on the Move Book Club rated it ★★★★★

A collection of poetry based on the life and loves of G.P.A. I have had the pleasure of reading his works before and it never tends to disappoint. Content that is moving, sexy, explicit, and all that in between you get a sense of who GPA is and how he feels and relates to certain situation. I am not a big poetry reader but it is something about his poetry that gives a story. You tend to visualize and feel his words.
Loved it and can't wait for more.
AAMBC Reviews

Nita Bee rated it ★★★★★
Shelves: august-reads

Simply amazing, is what I usually say when I read one of G.P.A's pieces and this book of poetic stories is no different. I was caught up and into it when I started the read. The poetry in this book was deep and moved me. I like the feeling G.P.A gave of personally speaking to me. It was like I was having a live conversation with him and I didn't want it to end. Maybe it was because I've watched him on his video's and could hear his voice in my ears while reading, I so love his style. I don't know but his words and his style are easy to fall in love with…he spoke truth, he spoke love, he spoke hurt…he was just speaking on the real and I loved it. There was definitely a taste of everything "life" in this book. You could tell he spoke of things he knew and from his heart.

Because I'm a lover of romantic love poetry, If I had to pick a favorite it would be "Tonight" in the "The Land of Multiples" section. If I had to describe that piece … Sensually beautiful…Romantic. Then again I guess I can describe all of them in that same section the same way. DAMN! But it doesn't just stop at that one section the whole book is captivating…you will begin 'til you come to the end and want him to speak more to you.

The Author's Corner shared Ubawa's Bestsellers's photo.
November 20

GPA is a prolific poet whose style of expression carries with it a rhythmic and quintessential undertone. *The Mind of a Poetic Unsub* is a work of poetry that takes you on an intimate excursion through almost every topic imaginable and known to man. I would highly recommend this book to book clubs or any individual who enjoys a good stimulating and fun read. Rating 5 stars.

Foreword

I am a fortunate man. Blessed would be an even more appropriate word. I have the pleasure, emphasis on the word "pleasure", to have been in the company of many beautiful, experimenting, and uninhibited women. Because I am a gentleman, there are no names that have been used in this book. That would be just too "Superhead" of me wouldn't it? Besides, if any of them read this book, they will know who they are. And that is the fun of it. The main character in this story is known to you, and that is me. Yeah, it is brazen, conceited, blah, blah, blah, but what do you expect from someone whose moniker is Greatest Poet Alive? Exactly. I do not want to do a lot of talking before you start reading, but there is something that needs to be said. If not at Poetry completely, then when it comes to love and sensual Poetry, I am the best!! Enjoy *Revenge of the Orgasm*. I sure did while creating the stories.

Always,

Unsub

15 Minutes

one minute to say hello and good to see you
two minutes to embrace you
two minutes to allow my eyes to travel your landscape, my nose to inhale your scent, touch your face and hair
one minute to compliment you, tell you how much I miss you and am glad to see you.
a minute to kiss your lips lightly
a minute to kiss your lips fully
a minute to kiss you and inhale your breath
a minute to kiss you and give you breath back
thirty seconds to pause
thirty seconds of looking into your soul and you mine.
two minutes to kiss you, exchange breaths, and let tongues salsa
a minute to hold your hand after kissing again
a minute to say I cannot wait to see you again, embrace and kiss you again.

Just give me fifteen minutes
Then, you can go back to work
Then, you can go back inside.
If you must, you can go back to him.

15 minutes

Lip Gloss and Undergarments

after dinner the walk was down Michigan Avenue
without provocation, she told him that she enjoyed
dinner, spending time with him
he answered but, knowing full well there was more
to her declaration
pausing then starting, her voice told him that
nothing further would come of them
stopping near Water Tower Place, he wanted more
clarity
asked her if that meant no kisses
yes, she answered
wanting to know then if her heart was not to be his
yes, she answered
and without him asking, told him that she would
never make love to him
he looked at her and smiled
stopping in front of her on the corner of Michigan
and Ontario, he said this

in the morning, when you get ready to leave out for
work
times after you have eaten, prepared for a date, or
just need to reapply,
allow me to be your lip gloss.

then without offense to your wishes, often could I
indulge your kisses
thin or thick would they be, but the frequency and
intensity, solely up to you
so if I cannot kiss you in this mortal form, then
allow me to so as your lip gloss
she giggled, and he kissed her quickly
her mouth open in surprise, he kissed her again
and continued

can appreciate your hesitancy when it comes to
your sacred place
you are, after all, a lady and never would want to
discover disgrace
nor would I wish or bring you to such dismal
depths
aware even more so that the place that keeps your
affection trust deserves
intentions of a higher purpose
so let me propose such

 I could make love to you constantly
thongs, boy shorts, g-strings, bikinis, and briefs
would denote all the positions we could entertain
the various colors would represent the various
backgrounds for all of it
close to you at all times, separated only when
bathing, showering, but still can watch

your orgasm at your summoning, for always would
I be on edge of chasm
at the same time that lower self occupied, beating
muscle would feel affection as well
two-fold tightly close so that not only am I shielded
from others' wavering eyes
but would also have my hands on your heart so
that you feel my affectionate touch

athletic, push up, full, halter, no matter
never would you have to question my motives
never would you have to wonder where I am
and if I could speak, I would tell you I am where I
want to be,
close to your heart
so if no love you wish to make with me or your
heart more worthy than being in these hands
then let me exist as your undergarments

she stood and looked at him

he smiled and shrugged
she then looped her arm through his as they
continued walking down Michigan Avenue
as they neared the bridge over the Chicago River
she laughed aloud and said, "Lip Gloss and
Undergarments"
he laughed

Comfortable

unfastened at the red light.

pulled through blouse at stop sign.

parked car, rolled up into a ball, and deposited in purse.

girls roam freely as she drives.

comfortable she is now.

Fortunate am I to have witness.

Obsessed

You have initiated indelible intimate indentations upon my intellect.

I only think of you in between the blinks of my eyes.

But I have told you a falsehood.

Every other heartbeat, you inhabit my mindset as well.

I am obsessed with you.

My dark skin contains odes written to you in various fonts.

Your favorite scent is what I use to freshen the air within and without my home.

The colors you have shown inclination towards are the paint on my walls, threads in my carpet, and tint of my wardrobe.

There are various pictures of you on my computer, within my phone, and in between the money and cards in my wallet.

I am obsessed with you.

My worst nightmares are fond remembrances of your idiosyncrasies.

Every prayer that my mouth utters contains gratitude to the Father for letting me be cognizant of your existence.

Easily have I memorized the rhythm of your footsteps no matter what shoes you are wearing, no matter the surface you are walking upon.

Collectively and separately, your initials and measurements form passwords and the combination to my locks.

I am obsessed with you.

And I know what you are thinking.

It is supposed to seem extreme.

It is supposed to come across as overkill.

It is supposed to make you feel a tad frightened.

If it were otherwise, it wouldn't be obsession.

I am obsessed with you.

I am obsessed with you.

I am obsessed with you.

Chocolate, Powdered Sugar and Strawberries

The strawberries were large and cool.
Powdered sugar was abundantly spread over the strawberries
Warm was the chocolate because that is the scent it gave off.
She licked, licked, licked, and licked the sugar from the strawberry's skin
Her teeth took a bite of the cool strawberry, and the juice tasted her lips, which her tongue wiped away.
Then with her spoon, she scooped some of the warm chocolate onto her plate, dipping her strawberry into it fluently.
What a combination...

The chocolate meshed with the strawberry, upon her lips coated with powdered sugar
And with aggressive intent, I watched
After she finished her third strawberry, her gaze captured mine.
She asked what I was thinking.
Again, I chuckled.

In another universe or another date, I would have told her the truth.
The length and width of me was supposed to be the sugar she licked off
My undercarriage and neck would be the strawberries she bit into
And opposed to her dipping chocolate, I would dip, delve into her

Discretion overcame bravado
I said none of that
Besides, it was just our first date...

Take a breath…now.

Enough

Beautiful woman is wearing a black, Donna Karan dress that was long but short enough.
My thumb is short but was found to be long enough.
She sat demurely like a lady would; her legs were spread wide enough.
Thumb did not enter fully, yet it made geometric shapes, occasionally grazing seventh letter spot, and causing chasm to drip nectar, so I guess thumb had delved deep enough.
Her moans were inaudible to all around us; however, I could hear them clearly and discern my name as she spoke it, and this told me they were loud enough.

In a reversal of fortune, my pants were affixed around my waist with belt pulled tightly, but obelisk found freedom because she had pulled zipper down enough.
Nowhere near a granite state, still brown skin turned purplish while vein protruded prominently, so I was hard enough.
Not on her knees, yet she was able to inhale and exhale, descend and ascend upon my appendage showing she had room enough.
Apex arrival had not yet, but eyes saw back, top, and front of brain, breath became scarce, and tumescence began to make its appearance, signaling that I was close enough.

As the taxi weaved through downtown Chicago, it turned onto the ramp to the Outer Drive.
The cab driver ignored all that was going on in his backseat.
It would seem the twenty dollar tip I gave him at the beginning of the ride...
Was enough

Extreme

Dark, lurid thoughts invade my mind; it is surprising I think of these things.
Dreary day outside of this Wisconsin Dells' cabin, your body stretched in four different directions, ass naked you sway to and fro in this erotic swing.
Painful ecstasy comes from moans as tighter it closes the nipple rings.
Restrained legs perform grasshopper movements from the pleasure the agony brings.

Hands become a paddle and a whip respectively reddening your backside repetitiously.
Gag in your mouth, blindfolded but still you scream out and stare directly at me.
Hot candle wax, melting ice, and sweet honey form outer layers of your skin.
Fully drenched and dripping your chasm, so I push swing forward, catch it when it comes backwards, then roughly I enter in.

Remove gag but breaths still find difficulty escaping.
Belt tightens around your neck, as the camera continues taping.
Lovemaking of a gentle sort was not your wish; you demanded more of an extreme.
The mask lowers over your face; now only you can hear your screams.

Westin Incident

The remote lowered the volume on the television.
Her screams are my ears' preference.
Several minutes have expired as I pause to withdraw.
Reprieve last mere moments, for the waters from her provide inspiration.

Three fingers plunge deep and return differently.
Saturation dripping is strategically placed upon ignored entrance.
A not so gentle smack across her buttocks signals and commands her readiness.
Magnificent landscape of hers releases a deep sigh, while her muscles tense then relax.
She is bent over this wooden table, her dress at her waist, and no other garments apparent.

Easing past initial barrier, adjustment occurs from cavern's and traveler's parts.
Grunts signify that halfway is now the journey.
Soft voice pleads for tortoise pace.
Dastardly, deliberately, and diabolically quickening denies the request.

Initial reaction is cursing and crying.
But the steady rhythm soothes assimilation to the discomfort until it no longer exists.
The table and her body move in synchronicity.
When her body moves, synchronicity is the table's response.
Synchronicity is the existence of the table and her body.

My hands rest with gentle pressure upon the small of her back.
It provides splendid sightseeing that includes the contours of her back, shoulders, neck, and hair.
While her forbidden cove held me warmly, my head turns toward the window.
Hoping that someone might catch glimpse of us; window had been purposely left agape.

Thrusts are focused on touching vaginal from this side
But my concentration's eye sees an intriguing sight on the other side of hotel, where the curtain is coincidentally pulled back.
A striking woman of opposite skin with lengthy, blonde hair is straddling a man who is only visible by his lower self.
From what I could tell, she smiles widely as her back arches and blonde mane whips violently.
My body now wears chills all over itself, while sweat has become its overcoat.
Velocity had already attached itself to my thrusts; ferocious now joins the description.

Simultaneously, my counterpart's gyrations become wilder; her facial expressions of ecstasy are discernible from this distance.
It seems that we are unison, in the same place, and switching positions.

She is on top of me, then I move myself behind her.
As the time travels its course, we are urging each other towards cataclysmic climax.
Our partners are oblivious, as if they are not present.
Muscles further flex and tense.
Faces twist into unrecognizable shadows of themselves.
Teeth clenched, while voices escalated.
Slightly ashamed, I arrive at my destination first.
When she joins me a few moments later, her collapse shows that satisfaction and she had met.

After our breaths were caught, we met at the window.
Smiling our waves, we pulled the curtains closed.

Pictures

Pictures
She enjoys taking them.
Pleasure mounts with the sharing.
And she does so often.

Menagerie manipulates mindset.
Arousing assortment asks attention
She shows her toes, nails, and smile just to tease.
Partial nudity makes one wish to see more.
But that privilege is reserved.

Late night, in the inbox, social network, or technological camera, she provides a show.
Poses run the gamut, while smiles accompany each.
Silly question she asks, knowing the answer.
Do I like?
I concede the obvious until she retires, leaving me with images that become beautifully, tortuous remembrances.

Pictures
She likes to take them.
Even more, she enjoys sharing.
With me, she likes to share them all.
And I appreciate it, when pleasure is left to my own devices.

Trail To a Pile

White low cut blouse
Crème colored skirt with lengthy slit above the left knee
Chain link belt
Crème-colored, four inch heels with red bottoms
Pink lace boy shorts
Bra matching the above
Clinique Happy perfume
Pearl earrings and necklace

Black slacks and coat
Purple long sleeve dress shirt
Black dress socks
Ferragamo black dress shoes
Sean John Unforgivable cologne
Black boxers
Black tee shirt
Giorgio Armani glasses

None of these things are being worn at the moment.
They are a lengthy trail.
A lengthy trail leads to large pile.

The Devouring (Haiku)

Ravenous hunger
Top of bald head visible
More she fed me

Fog

On a downward torrent, streams invigorating water.
Its baptizing touch is all encompassing.
Condensation develops, grows, and spreads its dominion.
Even in the dense and ever thickening steam, forms are recognizable.

With closer introspection, human they are.
Bodies can be seen interlocking, linking, and moving.
Two shadows become one.
The steam's tangibility heightens, thus providing discretion for those on the other side of it.

Sextet

Yellow icing covers a chocolate cake.
Translated from a literal, vivid description of a colorful sundress over a brown body.
Palms planted deep into sand caressed by water.
Sun's heat reiterates its superiority by extending to her posterior.
I am now an eclipse.
A breeze creates harmony between land, water, and sun.
And I wonder by us joining them and making it six, have we encouraged nature's wrath.

Her Flow

Time slows, halts, and speeds up.
The planet we exist upon spins off its axis.
Tremors touch terrain tearing it simpler than sharp
knives through wet paper.
Waves raise themselves to the height of skyscrapers
and mountains, splashing upon land, obliterating homes,
and drowning several.
From the cracks in the Earth, fire springs forth after the
water has passed.

This is not Revelations realized.
Nor has the Apocalypse arrived.
The world is not meeting its end.
And there are no natural disasters occurring.

I am in the embrace of her arms and thighs.
Equilibrium is dizzy from womb's whirlwind.
Obelisk's body is drowning in tsunami's torrent.
This is her flow.

Reprieve (Grab a second breath)

Midnight

Midnight awaits in the near distance.
Standing between two running vehicles are we.
Brown eyes look into twins.
The words spoken are kisses.

Resuscitating life, tongues dancing, time slowing kisses.
Even though coats cover, the heat of testosterone and
estrogen burns at the connection of bodies.
Hands travel with sense of direction with no singular
destination.
Hardening and moistening appear at the provocation.

A moment we breathe our own breaths.
Twins look into souls deeply.
Cars are still running.
And as the snow and temperature falls, people inhabit
the nearby Fred and Jack's eatery.
Midnight has made a cameo and departed.
We have not noticed.

Her Garments

She wore...
A Guess Zig Zag sweater
The jeggings that cover her lower self are Guess as well.
High heeled boots were manufactured by Stuart
Weitzman and jet black.

The thought of this combination was overwhelming.
My dark skinned face turned crimson at my cerebral
tangent.
From sweater to boots and all underneath, my wish is to
be them.

Monica

Monica
Favored to behold, curvy and voluptuous to a fault, teasing perfection.
Monica
Smile coated with effervescence and similarly that was arousing on its own merit.
Monica
Natural scent emanating jasmine and the advent of Spring. Yet, the aromatic aura that surrounds her is Hanae Mori.

Monica
Prone to giving light to clothes of various colors, but in my presence, her garb is all black.
Monica
Chanel sunglasses, leggings fitting snugly. She wears a blouse with a peek of magnificent cleavage, along with high heeled shoes or boots, thong fighting for existence in ample backside.

Monica
Her whispers conjure commands of a siren. Speaking voice emits octaves beyond my ears ken. Yet, it is quite soothing.
Monica
Though she is a fashionista, considers herself overdressed in thongs or boxers but prefers to be clothed

in nothingness. She sees nothing wrong with prancing around in such a state; and when the idea of her skin not being soft and shiny she stops and moisturizes.

Monica
Prone to sharing gentle, slow, soft kisses. Has an affinity for Riesling with her meals and waking to a latte. But her preference was for things of a roughly, violent nature. Choking, grabbing, smacking, toys, chains, raucous, maniacal, continuous, fast, and cataclysmic are just a few denotations.

Monica
Liked, loved, and lusted for her.
Everything a man could desire.
But we have never met in person.
Conversation over social networks, exchanging numbers, and text messaging of a casual and carnal nature.
But it was the pictures that provided provocative mindset

Monica…
One name

Six letters
Three consonants
Three vowels
Monica

Striptease

Dressed in Brooks Brothers blue pin striped suit, white
long sleeved dress shirt, red tie, and Bally shoes.
Business is over for the day, time to settle down.
Coat and slacks never made it to their hanger.
Shirt lands near hamper for washing.
But the shoes are fitted with shoe trees, placed in
sleeves, and returned in the closet.

White tee shirt is removed, while boxers stay on for now.
Five singles, ten fives, two twenties, and a debit card
with four hundred dollars are placed in my boxers.
There is no loud music.
No one else was there to see my act, me taking my
clothes off.
I strip for her

Yawn

Perhaps it comes from fatigue, boredom, or the affect of someone else.
It is no matter.
When it appears, her mouth barely opens.
No sound escapes.
Swift is the reaction of her hand to suffocate those eventualities.
After the movement occurs, the moment is gone.

Her Tattoos

Shoulder hosts a butterfly
Dragon dwarfs her back.
Calligraphy is written upon her right shoulder, which is
an ode to her mother.
Puerto Rican flag with hands surrounding stretches from
her cleavage covering her left breast.

Under her belly button is written Heaven in old English.
Roses with thorns circle her right ankle.
Vibrant colors cascade all over.
My kisses join the menagerie.

Her Feet (in My Hands)

In a tee shirt of mine, she relaxes in the chair.
Two basins, one is filled with warm water and the other soapy water.
I am armed with two wash cloths, towel, and my hands, all necessary for my pleasurable task.
I begin with her right foot.

Wash cloth dipped into warm water, then soaking her foot fully.
I followed by dipping second wash cloth into the soapy water and lathering right foot.
Then, I take her foot in my hands then dry it with the towel.
With similar deliberateness, the steps are repeated to the left foot.
And once they are both cleansed, I kissed them both.

With the washing and drying done, I retrieved her favorite lotion from Bath and Body Works.
This time, the treatment begins with the left foot, followed diligently by the right.
Now that her feet have been washed, dried, and moisturized, my fingers massaged all the aches of the day away.
And when I look for her approval, it is given by her slight snore.

Carnal Conversation

Warm and moist she said it was.
Touching herself with fingers pretending they are mine.
Soft moans are harmonious hums.
Her thumb presses pussycat's purr lightly then applies more pressure.
Yes, is the sentence she speaks.

After pressure is lessened, she draws her own circles.
Again appears the pressure, then there are more circles.
Water fills the chasm's composition.
Her breathless proclamation confirms this.

Two fingers slide in and out.
Slowly, slower still is the way they enter and exit.
Then steadily the pace quickens, but pivotal point is ignored for now.
Motions are similar to seconds ago; however, no spot is touched, given pause, and is touched again.

She bellows her pleasure, and then abruptly, she announces she must leave.
Her husband has come home and summoned her.
I leave my inbox on the social network and continue writing.

Depiction (Her Lips)

They look like a delicacy covered in expensive gloss,
killer lipstick, or their natural essence.
Simple smile, knowing smirk, or twisted into an alluring frown
Speaking sweet somethings or saying silence.

Kissing my baldhead
Kissing from the top to the bottom, and all in between
Kissing my birth, my existence, and my afterlife
Kissing me, kissing me, kissing me
With those lips

Tumescence

Taste of Chocolate

Her concentration rivals an assassin's.
A heightened frenetic is the speed of her motions.
She aspires to remove all of the powdered sugar and
warm chocolate from the juicy strawberries.
But in this realm, only chocolate exists.
Dark, rich chocolate it is.
And it just happens to be my skin.

Forbidden Dance

Dark skin, deep pitch as if it could be called night.
Eyes blue from the insertion of contacts
Curves on a highway are the description of her lips, hips, breasts, and backside
Voice soft with a slight squeak but not annoying
Poetic predisposition possessed her
Clothes clung because they had no choice

Met her not knowing who she was
Voice called my name and turned me around
Had spoken to her, tried not to stare with extreme difficulty
Sun glasses removed showed eyes I wanted to dance in
But to another per vows she belonged to
And I too promised faithfulness to another
Thoughts and wishes did not care

Too many glances
Too many chuckles
Too many purposeful, accidental touches
Too many interactions on phone and otherwise
Too many days and nights ignored by spouses

Dressed in all white made more pure and vibrant by her dark skin
A Saturday evening and night became opportune
Only moments of silence existed
Her body carried in my arms and laid upon awaiting bed

Though frenzied the pace, the motion was methodical.
A fruit with skin, I peeled each layer.
Hunger dove in before instrument of lust; easy it was to languish on the delicacy.
In the dark with a woman composed of darkness, meshed with my own to complete trilogy
With every bite, every grope, every lick, every thrust, even after she returned to him, confident everything of hers belonged to me.

Difficult it became to be away, regardless of prudent or sinful circumstance
Hypnotic tango the music between her legs dictated, so to its rhythm I went
A Friday evening provided opportunities rare
In all black, brazen by pulling vehicle in front of my domicile, she came.

Kisses were composed of hunger and thirst.
Drive to clandestine and sordid location was abrupt.
Second floor near back of hotel where our encounter would occur
Two twenty-three was the room number, ironic because it is the same number of my daughter's birthday

Instructed not to leave marks this time because he had questioned her, but still she wanted me to be brutal.
In my compliance, bulky belt buckle beat bountiful backside, large plastic bag over her head to reach orgasm without breath, and exhausted every inch of large room and each moment of the four hours.
Caught our breaths and felt each other's planets in the truck before she dropped me off.
It would be the last time we would see each other.
But how I remember the times we danced.

Tracing

A compromising position she was not supposed be in but needed to be.
Using good sense would have been prudent, but the urges overruled.
In a quandary, with mind set upon not sinning, heart beating in the midst of its own tug of war, and all the while, the flesh ran with idea illuminating itself.

From the right corner to the rise of her lips slowly
Dragging from the rise to the left corner
Then, quickly back to this journey's beginning
Over the underneath at a snail's pace continued the adventure
This travel alternated between the quick and slow, allowing the moisture and anticipation to grow.
And on all three points of this triangle, it did.

Complimented several times over about her lips
They are ample, pouting, and succulent.
So to avoid obtaining a letter of a scarlet nature, she held me in manicured fingers and traced her lips.
Both of them…

The 59th Street Metra Adventure

5:19pm, the rush has just begun in Chicago.
Commuters leave the incoming trains, board trains, walk to cars to drive away, or wait for rides that have not yet arrived.
She and I are neither of those.

5:22pm, the vehicle is positioned so that its exterior and downward position provide anonymity for her.
But my vision captures everything around me.
And while my body continues its movements, by anyone and everyone that glances this way, I can be seen.
I do not care, nor do I stop.

5:25pm, small crowds of two or three people gather and move on.
Some have even tried to move closer to our proximity to be sure of their assumptions.
As they approach, my smirking face meets them.
Some retreat, while some hold their positions, shaking their heads in feigned horror, giggling at our bold natures, and perhaps themselves becoming aroused.

5:30pm, a black 2011 Nissan Maxima speeds towards Stony Island heading south.
Laughter fills the vehicle, along with Janet Jackson's Moist.
How exhilarating it is to be watched.

She, Her, and Me

She spoke with disinterest on her face and a fake tone of enthusiasm on the phone.
Still don't understand why she answered.
Mischief overcame my mental.
And the look on my face, removal of my glasses, and slithering towards her caused a smile to cross her face.

Slid mini-shorts under, over, and off voluptuous frame
Kisses along inner thighs caused alteration in her voice's delivery.
Lips locked lips lower producing abundant aroma and significant moisture that follows.
Her speech on the phone now slurred.

Fingers first find my bald head, squeezing intensely, and leaving nail upon scarce follicles.
Phone is now on speaker; the female voice can be heard asking the happenings.
Squeals, moans, and whispering syllables give her the answers she seeks.
Feast has provided more than sufficient arousal for both of us.

Breaths are exchanged between the three of us.
Fingers lock pectorals, embrace breasts, and provide own stimulation.
The spread widens and is filled.
Entry is welcomed, while thrusts are given and returned.

Over the phone, no longer are questions being asked.
Audible now are gasps of satisfaction being searched for.
These are further accentuated by vivid, verbal descriptions of actions.
Faintly, sensual sounds can be deciphered.
A war is waged to determine who is experiencing more pleasure.
Is it me, she, or her?

Seems as though we are all in the same room, until the phone hangs up
This is only noticeable because it rings again.
And this time, it goes unanswered.

The Merging of Saturday into Sunday

11:45pm
Waking from evening nap
Much needed reprieve for carnal continuation
You stir as I do
Eyes on the same body clock
Realization removes cloudiness
You move towards me
As I reach for you

11:50pm
We are the state from which we were before
Slumber overtook us
Makes for erotic expediency
With no regard for anything
We continue

11:53pm
Your aggression comes to the fore first
My wrists you hold in your left hand
Out of the way
Placing my legs firmly together
Lifting obelisk and inserting
Leaning forward you kiss me
Moving posterior to a rhythm unknown to me
A rhythm not known to me
Can only feel the rhythm that is unknown to me

11:56pm
Slowly, tortuously the vertical movements
Then, like adrenaline seeped into your pores
Faster
Harder
Harder
Faster
Still holding my wrists
Your head bowed against my chest
Teeth finding and leaving their mark
Piercing skin
Piercing screams
Piercing upward movements myself accompany yours downward
Piercing

11:59pm
Breaking free of your restraints
I pull you close
Kissing you to breathe your air
Hand full of your hair
Maniacal is the intensity
Headlong, headlong into orgasmic oblivion

12:21am
Saturday has merged into Sunday
Showing no signs of halting

I would like to thank God for watching over me, blessing me, forgiving me, and making me special and talented. There are no words of admiration, love, and respect that I can speak to my Livingston crew. Shirley the Boss, Gus the Capo, Morgan the Future, and Scooter the Protector, you all mean the world to me. And every day is not the same day because of the experiences we share. Love you all. To our respective and respected families, Lester, Stennis, Taylor, Martin, Strahan, Moore, London, and James, thank you to everyone for having my back and giving your support. Family supersedes everything. Kottyn Campbell, thank you for being a great partner. Mary Rogers, thank you for showing and telling what friendship is. Real 'ish. I would like to thank all the members of #teamGPA for seeing a winner and rolling with him. I will never let you down again!!

This book is dedicated to all of the women that made these stories possible.

www.iblowyourmind.net

Pose (For Me)
she is not a supermodel.
no, not even close.
the manufactured superlative would insult her greatly.
the connotation that oozes from it goes against her
physical phenomenon.
she likes to pose.

the slender near anorexic figurines have nothing in
common.
cameras fail with their lenses to capture every admirable
aspect.
each and every curve on her has a mind, heart, and life of
its own.
parallel lines and ninety degree angles do not exist upon
her landscape.
an adventure occurs with every step of her feet.
she likes to pose.

she is at work, either bored out of her mind or close to
being stressed out.
exchange of pleasant salutations and developing
dialogue inspire inhibitions to depart.
business blazer top two buttons are placed behind suffix
skirt that coordinates pulled to expose the dark triangle.
done in privacy of her office, her car before she drives
off, or lunchtime sitting at her desk with everyone gone,
she likes to pose.

late in the evening, night knocks on the door.
there is privacy, whether created or existing.
garments clothe the floor surrounding her.
restraint acts as though it does not exist.
every inch made known that was otherwise; sure camera struggles grasping.
she likes to pose.

pedicured toes, tattoo around ankles.
curve of thighs respectively v leading to chasm, belly button, undersides, and posterior's arc nipples, swell of buxom bounties, delectable neck, succulent lips, tender shoulders captured in various lights, different angles, and no filters
she likes to pose.

staring at my catalogue of photographs.
at any time, arousal can be summoned.
Venus' machinations are of course superior to Martian mentality.
my full attention she has, and she knows it.
that is why, she likes to pose
for me

Createspace
100 Enterprise Way Suite A200
Scotts Valley, CA. 95066
www.createspace.com

A subsidiary of Amazon.com

"Revenge Of The Orgasm" - Copyright © 2013 G.P.A.
(Greatest Poet Alive)

All Rights Reserved, including the rights to reproduce this book or portions thereof in any form whatsoever. For information address Createspace 100 Enterprise Way Suite A200, Scotts Valley, CA 95066

This book is the work of fiction. Names, characters, place, and incidents are products of the author's imagination or used fictitiously. Any resemblance to actual events or locales or persons is entirely coincidental.
No part of this book may be reproduced, stored in a retrieval system, or transmitted by any means without the written permission of the authors.

Manufactured in the United States of America

www.ingramcontent.com/pod-product-compliance
Lightning Source LLC
Chambersburg PA
CBHW061512040426
42450CB00008B/1583